# REMARKABLE ABCS

N H A S E A M I O G
X                   D
J REMARKABLE N
N                   U
H D O A N M ABC S

KRISTIN PERSONS

Palmetto Publishing Group
Charleston, SC

*Remarkable ABCs*
Copyright © 2018 by Kristin Persons
All rights reserved

First Edition

Printed in the United States

ISBN-13: 978-1-64111-143-0
ISBN-10: 1-64111-143-7

# REMARKABLE
(re-mark-able) adj.

Worthy of being or likely to be noticed, especially as
being uncommon or extraordinary.

To my A, B, and C,

It's been *remarkable* . . .

# REMARKABLE

I thought I was ready to put this down,
to contain the damage we had already done,

But just as easy as it is to drive recklessly down
familiar roads,
I found myself back in your arms,

knuckles white, my grip tighter than ever—

and letting go is unimaginable.


For this moment, even if just for this moment,
holding on is *remarkable.*

# MUSCLE MEMORY

You roll over until your whole body is on top of mine.

"This is how I'm going to sleep," you say playfully, legs locked around mine, arms braced around me.

"Oh, really?" I tease. "OK then," and I slip my legs out from under yours and wrap them around you to keep you right where you are. I close my eyes.

"I definitely *cannot* sleep like this," you say into my neck with a muffled laugh. "It makes me want to do other things." You thrust your hips toward mine, the most blatant of hints.

Our laughter spills out into the dark, and I tighten my grip. "What doesn't make you want to do other things?" My question is lighthearted and accusatory.

We are a knot of limbs and giggles in a pitch-black room.

Your lips find mine effortlessly—as if by memory—and even though I can't see a thing, I can tell you are smiling.

3

# MARCH 22, 2018

Six years ago, you and I walked down opposite sides
of the same street still strangers,

Not the slightest bit suspect of the universal
conspiracy that had delivered us to that moment,

unable to know everything that would come after.

In the one instant that my friend raised her hand to
wave and took a step off the curb in your direction,

everything changed.

It was the proverbial pebble that sent ripples out into
still waters.

To this day, I float in its now subtle, rolling wake
at the will of a simple moment that has long since
passed.

# SERIOUSLY

What I love most about you is that you let me be
ridiculous.

While others have been uncomfortable with my
simple amusement and playful curiosity,

you have never once rolled your eyes.

Instead, you look right into mine and entertain
the silliest of my thoughts with the most serious of
consideration, your response twice as ridiculous and
wholly sincere.

# PERHAPS

We danced around it for a long time,

flirting with the idea, neither of us willing to make
the move.

Other people would point it out, poking fun at how
we'd perk up at the mention of each other—

but we would laugh nervously,
claim it was nothing,
cling tightly to the roles we had created.

The truth is, it was always a thought.

Perhaps my hesitation then was something inside of
me knowing that I would enjoy having you far too
much to ever stomach the consequences of letting
you go.

# I THINK I
# LOVED YOU

I think I loved you.

And maybe not in the way you love someone when
you spend most of your days together or when you've
known each other for years.

I don't know how you take your coffee.
I don't know how you handle a bad day.
And I don't know what you look like first thing in the
morning.

But I know how you smirk when I say something
funny.
And I know that whatever it is I do say will be met
with an effortless retort and our conversation will
flow. *In the easiest way.*
And I know that you make me feel brave and special,
like the very best version of myself.
And the way you look at me . . . well, I think maybe I
make you feel the same way.

Because the way you look at me, I have never been looked at like that before.
It is the safest I have ever felt.

So, no, I don't know how you take your coffee.
And I don't know how you handle a bad day.
And maybe I will never know what you look like first thing in the morning.

But I think I loved you.

# DAYDREAM AND YOU'LL MISS IT

*He'll have dark hair and light eyes.*
*And he'll be tall. So much so that I'll have to tilt my head back to*
*look up into his eyes and stand on my tiptoes when we kiss.*

I had a lot of ideas of what "it" would look like.

Until I ran my hands through your light hair while
looking straight into your dark eyes, leaning in to
kiss you with my feet planted firmly on the ground

and "it" came out of nowhere.

# SLEEP

I feel myself come back to my body.
Slowly, I open my eyes and see a white ceiling.
I know exactly where I am before I even see the color
of the walls.
I recognize the smell, the comforter with no sheet,
the familiar feel of the pillow my head rests on.

I take my arm from underneath the covers to wipe my
eyes and turn my head to the right.
He's sleeping soundly, as I always find him when I
wake up minutes before the alarm goes off.

His hair is disheveled, and the scruff on his face is
lying every which way from the weight of his cheek on
the pillow.

Though he looks so peaceful, his brow is furrowed as
it always seems to be.
Like his guard is up even in his dreams.

The bed is shaking.
He bounces his leg in his sleep, too, I've discovered.

I contemplate reaching over to grab his thigh and ground it, but I don't want to wake him.

He's tired.

The kind that needs sleep.

And the kind that needs peace.

So, the bed continues to shake, and I can feel the corners of my mouth turn up into a grin just as the bed shifts slightly, and I know he has woken for just a moment—enough for his leg to come to a rest, his arm to graze mine as he brings it down from above his head, and for his torso to turn so that he's lying on his right side facing away from me.

His back is bare except for the occasional freckle and the impression of bunched-up sheets. I turn to my stomach and place my arm close enough to feel the warmth of his skin.

I can feel my blinks get longer as sleep returns to pull me away.

One sweet moment, and I'm gone again.

# ALL THE SWEETER

The things I remember are ridiculous—

shepherd's pie,
a Ralph Lauren outlet,
a gray shirt—

things seemingly insignificant among the landmarks
of our memory.

I don't doubt that you remember the walk we took,
the swing we shared, the kiss on the cheek as I left,
but I remember

what you ate at the pub while we all laughed about
bodies being wonderlands,
where you bought polo shirts in all of the colors I
didn't choose,
what you were wearing when you came to find me on
that last day.

I so enjoy walking down our memory lane, stopping to admire our big, defining moments,

but wandering the spaces in between makes my favorite trip all the sweeter.

# PLANES, TRAINS, AND TOUR BUSES

"Six states in seven days," you told me.

I remember looking at you with a sort of awe, like
you were a little bit nuts in a wonderful way.

And all week, I've been thinking about the airports
that are receiving you—
how lucky they are!
And all the airports sending you off—
I know too well how they feel.

You sent me a picture of the tour bus you're on,
and I imagine it gets to see the most authentic parts
of you. The you that is drunk with sleepiness, all
laughter and content, the you that falls into a bunk in
the middle of the night, body and mind exhausted.

And I wonder about the day that a plane or a bus or
a car brings you full circle once again, and we'll sit
together on a couple of stools and catch up over a drink.

Maybe kiss in that dizzying way we do.

And whether we end up in a room with the greenest walls I've ever seen in a house owned by a hippy couple named Ted and Barbara, or eating hash browns in bed at four in the morning, I want you to know—

although you have had your fair share of adventure out in the world,

I have found great adventure in you.

# REAL

When I think about you, I'm easily seduced by how perfect it all seemed.

There are times I even let my mind wander dreamily down a road where life would have let us hold on to that forever.

But would we have been able to protect our perfection if we had *really* gotten our hands on it?

Our favorite possessions are always precious until they succumb to their first scratch. And then we start to hold them loosely. Recklessly, even.

Perhaps what makes the story of us so remarkable is that it never had to suffer the impurities of being real.

# THEN, NOW, TOMORROW

It happened somewhere between

sixteen
and
nineteen
and
twenty-three
and
twenty-four

in the mess of those first butterflies, of holding hands
secretly on a dark road, of kissing for the first time on
a crowded dance floor, of sleeping side by side.

I don't know where exactly, but it did.

And looking back, it's no wonder that at twenty-five,
I care for you in a way that could fill all of the spaces
between then and now

with plenty left over for tomorrow.

# GIVING IN

I lay there, curled into his side, skin on skin.

*Just sleep tonight,* we decided.

I rested my head on his chest, my left arm flung across his torso. He ran his hand up and down my bare back, pulling me in while we drifted off to sleep.

I slid my leg over top of his, lying as close as I could get, listening to his heart beat hard in his chest and matching him breath for breath.

He let out a sharp sigh, and before I knew it, he was holding himself above me.

"I can't *not* do this," he said as he pressed his lips to mine, kissing me hard and giving in.

# MERCIFUL ECLIPSE

What a sweet surprise to have you show up on my
doorstep at 3:00 a.m.

I had no idea when I went to bed—a little sad, a little
heartbroken—that just a few hours later you would be
here

in my town,
in my house,
in my room.

That I would need you in a way I didn't even know,
differently than I needed you then.

You see,
when we met, I couldn't see anything but you.
And over the years, I have waited patiently for those few
midnight hours when your orbit realigned with mine.
But now, I am blinded by a different sun.
And though you are no longer the light, you are a
merciful eclipse.

# MISS ME

To put it simply,

what I want is to feel that you miss me.

# FAULT LINE

I remember when it shifted.

You had made a joke, and after we shared the laugh,
I looked at you and saw that you were already smiling
at me.

That's when I felt it.
As close to tangible as a moment can be.

"What?" you asked, holding my eye contact.

"Nothing," I said, still looking at you—refusing to
be the first to break gaze—knowing you knew exactly
what had just happened.

# SWEET DELUSIONS

"You know what my favorite memory of us is?" he asked, his hand resting on my leg, the other wiping water droplets from the outside of his whiskey glass.

I felt my body relax and take a satisfying breath at his casual use of "us," having feared for so long that it was all a figment of my imagination, that he and "us" were but a sweet delusion.

"What's that?" I enquired playfully, curious as to which moment he had picked.

Truthfully, it didn't matter what came from his mouth next, only that he had laid out our sporadic moments together over the last four years to look them over carefully and choose a favorite.

# IMPASSE

You text me drunk from somewhere across the pond,

asking what it is I want from this
as if we are in some alternate universe where what I
want can matter at all,

angry with me that I won't tell you what you already know.

And that is this:

You were the only one who had a choice,

and you chose.

For the both of us.

When you said, "I do,"

you said *you don't*

get to ask me what I want.

# POINT OF IMPACT

My eyes opened at the touch of your fingers softly
connecting the freckles on my shoulder.

"Your shoulders are so tan," you mused, gazing at
the sun I had gotten the day before.

Still facing the wall, I smiled.

A week ago, I couldn't imagine you reaching out to
touch me so casually in such an intimate way. At
some point, we crossed over.

In this new place, it's not so unimaginable.

Those freckles on my shoulders faded with the
summer, but your touch left a mark of its own.

You can't see the lines you drew on my skin, but it's
the first place to ache when I remember.

# CHARLESTON

Tell me,

when you think about Charleston—

do you think about me?

# BUT MAYBE

I've spent a lot of time wondering what would have
happened if we had kissed that day.

I've imagined every romantic cliché.

Surely, it would have been emphatic and defining,
a clear moment when before became after.

There was too much potential swirling around in the
inches between us to not combust had we moved any
closer.

*Maybe.*

Or maybe life would have simply gone on.

Maybe we would have felt nothing, high-fived, and
walked away,
sparing the masses
and those whom, I came to find out later, were
closely involved.

It's the not knowing; it's the idea that it could have changed the whole world as we've known it, completely. Or not at all.

But *maybe*.

# THE GAMBLER

I could spend days on end with you in this fort of
blankets

playing our secret game.

The one where I try to make my quiet stand, to keep
my body from reacting to your soft, precise touch,

but my breath hitches

and a smile escapes past my gritted teeth in anticipation.

You begin to roll away, and for a moment I think I
have won.

A sweet, or perhaps bitter, victory.

My lungs deflate at the thought of your retreat
but quickly find their breath again when your lips
curl up into a wicked grin.

I've never had anyone call my bluff the way you do.

# MATCH POINT

Sometimes, I think you actively try not to look at me.

Perhaps because you know what I'll see there when you do—

that I'll see your gaze last one second too long, the corners of your mouth on the verge of a smirk, all the things you're determined to keep to yourself.

All night, I felt the chill of your avoidance.

But in one almost imperceptible moment, you slipped up,

and the room went up in flames.

# I THINK

I still think about you.

I think about how different my life would be.

I think about the me so happy and content to spend a lazy Sunday afternoon with you.

I think about the you rolling your eyes when I say something you won't admit is funny, though we both know it is.

I think about our *almost* existence, how we were just a couple of choices away from someday looking back at the moment it *did* happen.

And how a lot of pain could have been avoided,

I think.

# MAGNETS

Apart, we are fine. We live our lives in our own directions.

That's how they prefer it.

But in the same space, something as involuntary as gravity pulls us together.

A small step here, another there. Close enough for one innocent exchange, and we're all tangled up again.

And so they try to position themselves between us
to obstruct our paths
to deter our connection.

But without fail, we close the gap.

Let them roll their eyes and sigh their disapproval.

We are a mess of magnetism.

# MIDNIGHT TOKE

It's 1:15 in the morning, and we're sitting on two metal folding chairs in the garage so you can smoke before we go to bed.

You make a gesture to offer it to me.

"No thanks," I say with a sleepy smile.

Sitting here watching you unwind, knowing that in just a few minutes we will climb the stairs and fall asleep together as I trace shapes on your back, is more than enough high for me.

# NOT IF, BUT WHEN, NOW WHERE

There's a picture of us the weekend I first felt there might be more to what I feel for you than friendship.

When your blond hair still fell loose right above your brown eyes and I had a mouth full of silver braces.

It was snapped midaction, genuine and in the moment as you ran up behind me, a marshmallow shoved in your mouth.

Sometimes when I look around at the mess we've created, I wish we could go back there. Start again. Navigate differently.

And other times, I'm not sure it would make a difference.

I think it was always coming to this; we were always going to end up here in the "after."

At some point.
Sooner or later.
Never a question of if, only of when.

It was too tempting of a fire.

But now the question is:

Where do we go next?

# HERE WE ARE AGAIN

My life turned upside down the first time we kissed.

And this time, when our lips met, it was shaken up
all over again with the realization that this chapter
was over, sweet as it was.

For a while, I believed nothing could compare to the
high I felt with you,

until the universe brought you my way again

and my eyes were searching the blue of yours for the
brown of his.

# COUNTRY ROADS, TAKE ME HOME

Everyone is singing in slightly different keys, arms wrapped around one another. Some are looking around, others are looking up to the sky or back on a moment. Everyone is holding a drink, midtoast.

I lean into you holding out an exaggerated note, waiting for you to laugh and shake your head and push back into me.

You do. My delight is obvious.

As you shift to face forward again and take a sip of your drink, I steal a glance out of the corner of my eye.

*Haven't we been here before?*

Sitting on this bench, by this fire, in *this* place?

It echoes a memory.

Looking around, I don't have to wonder why they say it's *Almost Heaven.*

# KISS ME

Kiss me thoughtless.
Kiss me clueless.
Kiss me senseless.

In the middle of my hesitation,
when I'm trying to hold on,
when I'm fighting the fall,

kiss me thoughtless, clueless, senseless.

When I'm thinking a million thoughts,
fighting every urge,
trying not to feel the heat of your skin,

kiss me thoughtless, clueless, senseless.

When I'm trying to make sense of things—
anticipating, fixing what isn't broken—
when I'm trying desperately to hold on to control,
to keep composure,

kiss me thoughtless, clueless, senseless.

Grab me and pull me. Use both hands, fill them with as much of me as possible. Smother all of the space between us and burn me with your skin.

And then kiss me thoughtless.
Clueless.
Senseless.

Breathless.

Until I let go.

# MORE SO

I hear from you every so often,
and though it's mostly

*Hi, how are you?*

And

*It's been a long time,*

I can still feel the weight of our shared "what if" on
the shoulders of our casual exchanges.

We are both happy in our separate lives, but there
will always be an awareness—one only we know—that
had we made a different choice, we could have been
just as happy.

Or maybe even more so.

# MUSIC

You insist on falling asleep with the TV on while I
desperately try to drown out the dim glow and noisy
dialogue.

But my annoyance melts away when, your eyes closed
and seemingly asleep, an unguarded giggle escapes
from your chest at something I must have missed,

and it is music to my ears.

# QUIET SHOUTING

I don't know if I've ever been mistaken for subtle.

Everyone knew.

It was in their sympathetic gazes
as excuses and explanations rolled off my tongue
dripping with adoration.

We all know you don't have to say things out loud to
be saying them loudly.

But, then again, maybe you do.

*Everyone* knew.

And yet I pray that you were just naively immune to
my blatant affection

because you would have been more careful with my
heart had you known.

You would have been more careful.

I *know* it.

Or, at least, I hope.

# WHY NOT ALWAYS?

In the middle of our best moments,
in the space between the last sigh of our laughter and
the look we share after,
I can't help but think,

*Why not us?*
*Why not this?*
*Why not always?*

It's in that look that I search your eyes for all of the
things you aren't telling me.

# JULY 21, 2017

You always need to play it cool and casual, unattached and without a care.

You can say you don't remember, you can say the whole night was a haze of smoke and booze, you can say whatever you need to say.

But I will never forget the way you looked right into my eyes, softly brushed the hair away from my face, and leaned down to kiss me—

slowly

and with all the care in the world.

# FORTIFIED

We once spent a whole week in a fortress of our own
making, spending all of our time together—

more time collectively than ever before.

On our first day outside of its walls, you said,

"I miss our bubble,"

and it was everything I didn't know I wanted to hear.

# PERSONAL

*It's nothing personal, just busy*

. . . is the phrase that broke my heart. It somehow turned all the things I've thought about us inside out, unrecognizable, like perhaps none of it was real. I must have imagined it all. For I have only ever regarded the things related to us as *personal.*

# SCARS

We both have scars.

Some we can see and some we cannot.

When we come together, the scars on our bellies touch and I like to think that the other ones, the ones we can't see, are touching too—familiarizing themselves with each other.

# NEXT TO YOU

You were so intent on making me watch a scary movie.

*A little played out,* I thought. *But why not?*

That night, lying in a dark room alone, still stirring
from the adrenaline,

I made a choice.

To grab my pillow and tiptoe down the hall,
open the door to where you were sleeping,
and climb into the space next to you,

leaning on a crutch of nervous laughter and "like hell
I'm sleeping alone."

Truthfully, I wasn't as afraid of the dark as I led you
to believe.

I was more afraid that if I let this obvious moment
pass, I would kick myself.

I had never slept comfortably in a bed with another
person

until I closed my eyes and opened them

still lying next to you. Rested and calm.

The kind of illusive calm that descends before a
storm.

# SNAPSHOTS

I don't have any pictures of you,
nothing to hold and look at,
no proof of our standing side by side.

But I have a picture of me looking at you,
taken by someone who knew exactly what was written
all over my face.

And maybe that serves as a better reminder of you
than any picture of us ever could.

# UNFORTUNATE TRUTHS

I know it's time to let you go,

to trust that whatever is meant to be will be,

but I'm scared to make that choice.

I fear that the moment I make up my mind

will be the moment you change yours.

And our moment will be missed.

# AMEN

I hooked my fingers into his front pockets as he planted a kiss on my lips.

An old, familiar song came through the jukebox, and still standing there together, we sank into a slow sway.

"I love this one," I said, humming quietly as we danced in the middle of the bar.

"You don't know this song . . . ," he challenged, pulling away, looking impressed and smiling as if to catch me in a lie.

His eyes willed, *Prove it.*

"Of course I know this song," I mused, feigning shock at his accusation before I leaned back into him, my lips to his ear, and sang each word clearly:

"If you ask me how long I'll be faithful, I'll be happy to tell you again. I'm gonna love you forever and ever, forever and ever . . . amen."

# Z .

I love you.

# ABOUT THE AUTHOR

An avid reader and dedicated learner currently study-
ing Education, Kristin Persons writes based on real-
life experience and aspires to share her love of words
through story-telling, in its various forms. She is in
pursuit of the sentence that makes readers close the
book for a moment and think, *That.*

Made in the USA
Middletown, DE
16 April 2019